DON'T TRUST A FART

FUNNY STORIES OF FLATULENCE AND REGRET

UPGRADED BOOKS

CONTENTS

ALSO BY UPGRADED BOOKS

LEGAL DISCLAIMER & WARNING LABELS

Let's be clear: this book contains tales of bodily betrayal, public humiliation, and fabric casualties. Reading may cause tears (the good kind), sudden realizations about your own near-disasters, and the irresistible need to share these stories with people who definitely didn't ask.

WARNING: Do not consume this material while eating chili, sipping coffee, or attending solemn events. We accept no responsibility for spit-laughs, table-slaps, or the sudden expulsion of bodily fluids.

MEDICAL DISCLAIMER: If you find yourself nodding in grim recognition, please consider talking to your doctor. Or your therapist. Or just buy stock in adult diapers and call it a day.

IDENTITY DISCLAIMER: All names and details have been changed to protect the truly guilty. Any resemblance to actual people, past or present, is purely coincidental – or hilarious.

You've been warned. Proceed with tissues. (For the tears. Probably…)

HOW TO USE THIS BOOK (A USER'S GUIDE FOR MAXIMUM EMBARRASSMENT)

Welcome. You've just invested in the most dignified way to lose your dignity.

This book was assembled not by scientists, but by people who made poor life choices and then shared them.

Best places to read this book:

- **Bathroom:** Let's be honest – this is what bathroom literature was invented for.
- **Coffee table:** A guaranteed way to make your guests rethink the friendship.
- **Waiting rooms:** Nothing eases the tension like chuckling at someone else's downfall.
- **Airplanes:** Because misery loves company.

Chapter map: We start small. Awkward. Embarrassing. And then we escalate – fast. By the end, you'll understand why trusting a fart is basically the worst bet you can make. Feel free to skip around and go straight to the stories that interest you the most; this isn't a novel.

Sharing rules: Great for...

- Bachelor parties
- Office gossip
- Sibling rivalries
- Family game night (if your family is cool)

Avoid at all costs:

- First dates
- Job interviews
- Religious ceremonies
- Anywhere the word "dignity" still means something

Like tequila shots or questionable leftovers, this book is best consumed responsibly.

Don't binge unless you want abdominal cramps.

Now relax. Laugh. Point fingers. It's okay.

This is how humans bond: by mocking each other's disasters.

INTRODUCTION

Every family has a story. Every workplace has a legend. Every circle of friends has *that one incident* that nobody forgets. The kind that lives forever in whispers, laughter, and lingering shame. This book is a collection of those stories – the moments when embarrassment reached Olympic levels.

The creed is simple: **Don't trust a fart.**

Say it slowly. Let it sink in. It's the wisdom of generations condensed into four devastatingly true words.

Here you'll find the chronicles of people who believed they were safe, only to discover that biology doesn't care about your confidence.

These are people who rolled the dice on digestion and lost spectacularly. And while they may have forfeited their pride, they gained something else: a story that makes the rest of us feel a little less alone.

We've gathered them all here, told in one confessional voice – Alex, the poor sap who represents all of us. He's not one person, but every person who's ever muttered, "Oh no" in a crowded room.

So pour a drink. Take a seat. And prepare to laugh until it hurts. These stories are messy, human, and unforgettable – just like life. And if nothing else, remember this: when your gut whispers, "Trust me," *don't.*

1

THE TURBULENCE TANGO

Seat 12B. Middle seat. Seatbelt light on. Somewhere over Missouri, my stomach filed its own flight plan.

The day had started like a bad idea in a tortilla: airport burrito at 7:10 a.m., eaten fast at Gate C17. Now I was wedged between a snoring businessman and a grandmother working a crossword in pen. The seatback screen played fish gliding over the Great Barrier Reef. I envied them; free to swim away.

Pressure built. I told myself the usual lie: just a little gas. The businessman's shoulder pinned me from the aisle; the grandmother pursed her lips and wrote seven-letter words like a judge. I considered waking him and making a run for the lavatory, and then I considered my pride.

Turbulence hit. So did my decision. I tried the quiet option – like every fool who has ever trusted physics, luck, and a burrito.

It wasn't quiet. It wasn't small. *And it wasn't just air.*

Heat spread. My face did the same. The businessman twitched, nose alert. The grandmother froze mid-clue. For a second, we all listened, as if the plane itself could explain what had happened.

"Excuse me," the businessman said, still half-asleep. "Is the air conditioning... broken?"

I muttered an apology and stood. He shot upright, pressing himself into the armrest like it could teleport him. The grandmother slid toward the window and stared at the wing with religious intensity.

The walk to the lavatory was a ballet of small steps and one very large regret. Ten long minutes later, I emerged – one pair of underwear lighter, one lifetime of humility heavier. By some miracle, the seat fabric was clean. I thanked every god with a loyalty program.

I reached up for my carry-on, found the travel cologne, and gave a discreet spray. The grandmother glanced over her glasses; I offered a weak smile. Mercifully, she returned to 23-Across.

For the last half hour, I watched the news and pretended to be a man who needed only a shower, not a new identity. When we landed, the businessman avoided eye contact with the skill of a professional. Fair.

NEWS FLASH (from the Department of Painfully Earned Wisdom): Never trust a fart on a plane.

.   .   .

After-Action

Regret Meter: 9/10
Clean-up Cost: 1 pair of briefs + a
travel-size cologne.
What I learned: Start in the aisle seat.
Or start fasting.

Alex's airborne disaster didn't end the week.
Back on the ground, Helen met my parents.

2

THE IN-LAW INTRODUCTION

White carpet, new shoes, a neighbor's dog with bad manners. That's the whole forecast.

Helen arrived at my parents' place with flowers for Mom and a nice bottle for Dad. Dad loved the label, and Mom loved the peonies. Conversation warmed: work, gardens, weather. Helen exhaled. For twenty minutes, *perfect.*

Then the odor arrived – polite at first, then ambitious. Dad sniffed. "Do you smell that?" Mom's eyes narrowed, scanning the room like a smoke alarm.

Helen looked down. A brown comet tail streaked the immaculate white carpet. The source was obvious: tread from the front walk, courtesy of the neighbor's terrier. She blinked twice, then whispered, "Oh no."

"It's okay," Mom said, voice tight as piano wire. She disappeared and returned with gloves, spray, and towels that had never seen daylight. Dad hovered with the credit-card scraper, a veteran of household battles.

I fetched a trash bag and tried to help. The streak grew less comet, more cloud. Dinner moved to paper plates because, as Mom put it, "the good china doesn't need to be part of this memory."

Helen apologized every third breath. Mom kept saying, "It happens," in a tone that suggested it should never, ever happen here again. Dad calculated the square footage as if it owed him money.

A week later, a receipt arrived for professional cleaning, along with a polite note proposing future dinners at restaurants. *Fair again.* My parents warmed to Helen eventually – six months, three dinners on neutral turf, and one shoe-check at the door every visit.

Family name for it now: *The Great Carpet Catastrophe.* Helen hates the title.

She also double-checks her soles like a surgeon scrubbing in.

After-Action
Regret Meter: 7/10

Clean-up Cost: One professional carpet cleaning and a peace-offering dinner.

What I learned: At a white-carpet house, greetings can wait – shoes first. Check soles, ask the house rules, then hug.

House Rule: gifts at the door, shoes off on the mat, and always scan the lawn.

3

INTERVIEW INTESTINAL INCIDENT

Boardroom. Leather chair. Three managers across the table.

Across the table, they held my résumé like it contained state secrets.

Meanwhile, my gut was already sending distress signals, pounding out SOS in Morse code.

The morning had started responsibly enough. Oatmeal and fruit for fuel, two coffees to sharpen the brain, twenty minutes of meditation to calm the nerves. Everything felt dialed in. Except no amount of deep breathing prepares you for fruit that might have been just a little past its prime.

By the time the receptionist called my name and offered her corporate smile, my insides had already begun whispering their betrayal.

I took my seat. The panel was every nervous candidate's nightmare: the department head with a clipboard, the HR director with her evaluating stare, and a regional executive who looked like he could make or break my future with one raised eyebrow. Behind them, floor-to-ceiling windows framed the city skyline, as if even the buildings wanted to watch me squirm.

"Tell us about your experience with data analysis," the department head asked.

I delivered my polished response, trying to sound like a man in control. I talked regression models and forecasting trends while quietly begging my digestive system to settle down.

Instead, my stomach doubled down, knotting itself into what felt like a balloon animal convention.

"Excellent background," the HR director said with a nod. "And how do you handle high-pressure situations?"

The irony nearly killed me.

Because at that very moment, I was handling the highest-pressure situation of my entire life. Not the interview – my bowels. I shifted slightly in the leather chair, thinking a small, careful release might save me.

It wasn't small.

It wasn't careful.

And it definitely wasn't silent.

The sound was catastrophic – somewhere between a foghorn and a whoopee cushion in surround sound. Two seconds later, the smell confirmed the disaster. The regional executive flinched like someone had opened a mustard gas canister.

The HR director coughed delicately and suggested, "Perhaps we should... take a short recess?"

Translation: *Evacuate before we all perish.*

I mumbled something about water, bolted for the restroom, and performed a level of damage control that should qualify as emergency management training.

One pair of underwear sacrificed, one cloud of cologne deployed, one candidate now humbled beyond belief.

Walking back into that room required more courage than skydiving.

They smiled politely, and I smiled back, pretending nothing had happened, even though we all knew it had. We wrapped up with firm handshakes that felt less like professional courtesy and more like last rites.

Two days later, I got the email. "We appreciate your interest and wish you success in your future endeavors."

Corporate code for: *Please never darken our conference room again.*

NEWS FLASH: Never trust a fart in an interview. Especially not in leather chairs.

After-Action
Regret Meter: 10/10

Clean-up Cost: One suit fumigated, one ego demolished.

What I learned: Always know the bathroom location. And maybe fast before life-changing events.

While Alex was recovering from his professional humiliation, Helen was about to experience a public slip-up of her own.

4

THE SCIENTIFIC SLIP-UP

Not all disasters come from the digestive system. Sometimes your own mouth decides to betray you in front of a crowd. Listen to Helen.

Helen was a rising star in biology, invited to present at the Regional Science Symposium. The auditorium was packed with professors, researchers, and grad students – an audience she had been dreaming of impressing. She was calm, confident, and ready. Slides polished, laser pointer in hand, research airtight.

"Our findings show major acceleration in cell organism growth," she began smoothly.

At least, that's what she *meant* to say.

What came out was: "Cell *orgasm* growth."

The word echoed through the sound system like a gunshot in a cathedral. The room froze. For one long, terrible second, there was only silence. Then the first giggle. Then another. And then the kind of rippling laughter that no scientist ever wants attached to their life's work.

Helen's cheeks went scarlet.

She stammered: "I mean organ – organism – cellular organism."

Which only made it worse. Like pouring gasoline on a lab fire. The audience lost it, professors shaking with laughter, grad students whispering to each other with gleeful horror.

Somewhere in the front row, a distinguished professor had gone purple trying not to burst into hysterics.

And the worst part? Helen still had fifteen minutes left to present.

Every time she said the word "growth," half the auditorium twitched.

When the Q&A came, some joker raised his hand and asked about "reproductive biology applications." Deadpan. The place broke again.

By the time she staggered offstage, she wanted to throw her laser pointer into the sun.

Her paper eventually got published in a prestigious journal, but her new nickname among colleagues stuck around far longer than she had wanted. The symposium became legendary not for her research, but for the day science accidentally discovered cellular orgasms.

After-Action
Regret Meter: 8/10

Clean-up Cost: One career's worth of teasing.

What I learned: Mouths have a mind of their own. Science can be sexy, but maybe not like that.

Helen's verbal blunder became legend in the scientific community, but Alex was about to prove that a quiet yoga studio can be the right setting for a more... visceral kind of horror.

5

HOT YOGA HORROR

Hot yoga. Ninety minutes. One hundred and five degrees. Supposed to cleanse body, mind, and spirit. For me – Alex – it became the stage for one of my most humiliating public betrayals.

I'd been going for a few weeks, thinking I was finally getting the hang of it. The studio was bright and steamy, mats lined up like colorful little islands of optimism. Thirty people were already stretching, breathing deeply, and pretending they didn't care how sweaty they looked. The air smelled of eucalyptus, ambition, and the faint sour tang of too many water bottles.

Our instructor, Sarah, was the kind of calm, gliding figure you'd expect in a yoga commercial. Her voice was smooth, her posture perfect, and her presence oddly reassuring. She said things like "connect with your center" and somehow made you believe you had one. I looked around at the others – flexible, serene, glowing – and thought, *Yeah, I belong here too.*

That optimism lasted about thirty minutes.

The warmup went well. Triangle Pose? A little wobbly, but serviceable. Standing Head-to-Knee? Not elegant, but no worse than the guy in the back who looked like he'd been tricked into attending. For a while, I fooled myself into thinking I was getting flexible, maybe even spiritual.

Then came the balancing series.

Tree Pose requires standing tall, calm, and steady. My problem? My kale-and-quinoa lunch had decided to run its own inner yoga practice. Let me tell you: digestive chaos doesn't balance on one foot. I stared at the wall like Sarah instructed, but all I saw was a green salad laughing in my face.

Next came Bow Pose. You lie flat on your stomach, grab your ankles, and arch backward like a human rocking chair. Normally, this stretches your back and looks impressive. But when your insides are staging a mutiny, it becomes something far darker. The pressure built. I clenched, I prayed, I thought of anything except biology.

"Breathe deeply," Sarah said softly. "Open your heart."

I breathed. And something else opened.

The sound was unmistakable. Wet. Echoing. Loud enough that mats shifted and heads popped up across the room. In a 105-degree studio, the odor was immediate, swirling through the heat like a fog machine at the world's worst concert.

Thirty pairs of eyes registered the same thought: *Who did that?*

It was me. Alex. Trapped on my mat, unable to deny it, unable to disappear.

Sarah, bless her, handled it with saintly diplomacy. "Sometimes the body releases what it no longer needs," she said, her voice even, calm, professional. The yogis nodded like wise disciples. But the subtle scoots of mats toward the far corners of the room told the truth. Everyone wanted distance.

The last thirty minutes dragged like an eternity. My poses collapsed into survival stances. My mind screamed at me to leave, but my pride insisted on staying until the bitter end. I sweated, I suffered, and I stared at the ceiling tiles like they might open and beam me up.

When the final Savasana came, I lay flat on my back, pretending to meditate but really calculating escape routes. As soon as Sarah whispered "Namaste," I bolted. Straight out the back door, skipping the customary yoga chit-chat about chakras and breakthroughs. At home, I peeled off my ruined gear, stuffed it in the wash, and stood under the shower vowing never to trust kale again.

After-Action
Regret Meter: 9/10

Clean-up Cost: One yoga mat, one outfit, and one shattered sense of inner peace.

What I learned: Enlightenment is easier when your intestines aren't actively plotting against you.

Alex's hot yoga humiliation wasn't the only mess that week. Later, romance decided to betray him, too.

6

THE GRAND ROMANTIC GOES OFF-KEY

Yoga humiliation taught me humility. Romance taught me restraint. Or rather – it should have.

For our anniversary, I wanted to prove to Helen how much she meant to me. Dinner at her favorite Italian restaurant was just the start. My real plan? A surprise serenade. With a mic. And Whitney Houston's *I Will Always Love You.*

Yes, I thought that was a nice idea.

The setting was perfect: dim lights, soft chatter, candlelit tables. I gave my toast, heartfelt and shaky, and people leaned in, smiling indulgently at the sweet couple in love. Then I nodded to the staff, and the music started.

That's when it all unraveled.

My voice cracked like a teenager at choir practice. The high notes? Gone. The low notes? Wobbly. I sounded less like Whitney Houston and more like a nervous chihuahua who'd swallowed a kazoo.

Helen's face went on a journey: surprise, confusion, horror, and then that forced, frozen smile that screams, *Please stop, you're killing me.* The diners around us shifted uncomfortably. One guy stared deeply into his spaghetti as if it might rescue him. Another actually winced.

I soldiered through to the end, drenched in sweat, gripping the mic like it was a lifeline. The applause was thin, polite, and motivated entirely by pity. I sat down to find Helen staring at me with wide eyes and clenched teeth.

"Why would you do that?" she hissed.

Because I loved her. Because I was a fool. Because in my head, it sounded better than it did in real life.

To her credit, she didn't dump me then and there. Later, she admitted it was "sweet" – in the same way a puppy peeing on the carpet is "sweet." From then on, she made it clear: gestures of love were welcome, but keep them private. No more restaurant concerts. No more public Whitney Houston. Ever.

After-Action
Regret Meter: 7/10

Clean-up Cost: One anniversary dinner and one badly wounded pop anthem.

What I learned: Big gestures don't always mean big romance. Sometimes love is best whispered, not belted.

While Alex's romantic ambitions fell flat, his gut was preparing for another public performance in a much more confined space.

7

THE ELEVATOR INCIDENT

Elevators are supposed to be quick, simple, boring ... right?

You press a button, ride a few floors, maybe nod politely at a stranger, and then it's over. For me – Alex – one Tuesday morning turned that routine ride into a claustrophobic nightmare, complete with witnesses, judgment, and a burrito I will regret forever.

The day had started fine. Crisp shirt, knotted tie, shiny shoes. A client meeting on the twenty-seventh floor of a downtown high-rise. I wanted to look competent, professional, like a man who belonged in skyscrapers. Instead, I swung by a drive-thru and bought a breakfast burrito the size of a football. It was greasy, delicious, and warm in all the wrong ways.

By the time I joined the crowd at the elevator bank, the burrito was already stirring. Two women in sleek suits whispered about their boss. A courier balanced an avalanche of packages. Three sales bros in matching polos smelled like cologne samples. I stepped inside with them, hit "27," and leaned back against the mirrored wall like I had everything under control.

My stomach had other plans.

The first gurgle was deep. Ominous. I clenched, hoping it was nothing. But elevators have a cruel way of stretching time. Floor 9...10...11. Every number took forever, and every second gave my burrito more courage.

The first attempt slipped out before I could stop it. A sharp little betrayal that echoed far louder than physics should allow. I froze. The courier twitched his nose. The suits stopped whispering. One polo guy looked at me like I'd personally offended his family.

I kept my face blank. Poker face. Pretend you're as disgusted as everyone else. Maybe they'll believe it.

But burritos don't stop at one.

By Floor 14, the elevator was a crime scene. The smell rolled through the box like mustard gas in a shoebox. The courier pulled his shirt over his nose. One of the women coughed. Another just stared at the doors, whispering a prayer for escape.

And then the universe decided humiliation alone wasn't enough.

The elevator shuddered. Jerked. Stopped.

Between floors.

Silence. Then six heads turned toward me, in perfect unison, as if choreographed. They knew. Everyone knew. I wasn't just the guy in the elevator. I was the reason this small metal coffin suddenly felt uninhabitable.

A voice crackled over the intercom: "Maintenance is on the way. Estimated wait: ten minutes."

Ten. Eternal. Minutes.

I tried not to breathe. Tried to shrink into the wall. But there's no shrinking when the evidence is everywhere. Every cough, every sideways glance, every shuffle of feet reminded me that my breakfast burrito had turned me into the villain of this ride.

When the doors finally opened, it wasn't polite. It was a stampede. Everyone bolted like freed hostages. No nods, no goodbyes, just the thunder of footsteps and the sound of relief.

I stepped out last, straightened my tie, and walked into my client meeting smelling faintly of lobby air freshener and permanent shame.

. . .

After-Action
Regret Meter: 10/10

Clean-up Cost: One burrito ban, one lost
client, one ego flattened.

What I learned: Elevators magnify everything. Especially burritos.

Alex's elevator disaster wasn't the only humiliation that week. A pool party was waiting to
finish the job.

8

THE POOL PARTY INCIDENT

Pools are supposed to be fun. Sun, splashing, laughter, the air filled with the wonderful smell of burgers on the grill. But nothing ruins a summer afternoon faster than realizing you've accidentally turned yourself into the entertainment.

It was a friend's barbecue at his apartment complex. Everyone lounged by the water, drinks in hand, music playing from a portable speaker. I had two goals: eat three cheeseburgers and impress people with my cannonball.

The setup was perfect. The diving board glistened in the sun. People gathered around with curious smiles. Someone even shouted, "Go, Alex!" I strutted up like an Olympian, heart pounding, ego inflating.

One bounce. Two. Then I launched into the air like destiny itself had booked me for this performance. I tucked tight, braced for impact, and slammed into the water with all the grace of a meteor.

The splash was biblical. A wave surged across the deck. Cups went flying. Burgers drowned. Someone screamed. For a fleeting moment, I thought I was a legend.

Then I surfaced.

And realized my swim trunks hadn't surfaced with me.

Gone. Vanished. Ripped away by the combined forces of gravity, velocity, and chlorinated betrayal. The pool went silent, except for the filter humming in the corner. Then came the laughter – rolling, unstoppable, merciless.

I flailed underwater, searching desperately, but my trunks were gone to the deep. Finally, someone threw me a towel, the kind of mercy you only get from a true friend. I climbed out, dripping, clutching fabric around my waist while everyone else clutched their sides from laughing too hard.

The party carried on, but my reputation didn't. For months afterward, people introduced me at gatherings with, "This is Alex – the cannonball guy." Not exactly the legacy I'd been hoping for.

After-Action
Regret Meter: 9/10

Clean-up Cost: One pair of swim trunks, one ruined barbecue, and one legendary story at my expense.

What I learned: Cannonballs make waves. Some follow you forever.

The cannonball incident became the go-to summer story, but Alex was about to top it with a formal-wear catastrophe.

9

THE WEDDING RECEPTION INCIDENT

Weddings are supposed to be beautiful. Joyful. Emotional. They are not supposed to include the sound of me accidentally derailing a romantic moment with digestive thunder. But fate has a cruel sense of humor.

This particular wedding was lavish. Crystal chandeliers, a string quartet, white roses everywhere. The bride glowed, the groom cried, and the guests dabbed their eyes as the newlyweds took the floor for their first dance. It was picture-perfect. Until I joined the reception.

I'd been running late and hadn't eaten all day, so when I saw the buffet, I made a tactical error. I didn't pace myself. I piled my plate high with shrimp cocktail, stuffed mushrooms, and a suspiciously creamy pasta that should have come with a warning label. I wolfed it down, grabbed a second helping, and washed it all down with two glasses of champagne. I thought I was celebrating.

Really, I was prepping for disaster.

The trouble began during the toasts. Everyone stood, clinking glasses, listening to heartfelt words about love and family. I sat there, smiling, pretending to be moved. Inside, my stomach churned like a slow-turning cement mixer. By the time the best man made his joke about "ball and chain," I was sweating.

Then came the slow dance. The bride and groom swayed gently to the music, and the crowd circled around them in a quiet, reverent hush. This was the moment everyone would remember. A magical snapshot of love.

And then – me.

I shifted my weight, trying to relieve the pressure, and lost the battle. The sound was impossible to ignore. It blasted across the polished dance floor like someone had stepped on a duck with a megaphone.

The music kept playing, but the mood was shattered. Guests stifled giggles. Someone gasped. The bride shot me a look that could have turned water into steam. The groom tightened his grip on her, as if shielding her from the evil in our midst.

I muttered something about "the floorboards" and tried to shrink into my chair. No one bought it. The laughter bubbled, spreading from one corner of the room to the other, until the carefully orchestrated romance was replaced with snickers. The bride would never forget her first dance – but not for the reason she deserved.

When the song ended, the couple retreated quickly, and the DJ cranked up something loud, mercifully covering further humiliation. But the damage was done. For the rest of the night, every glance in my direction carried the same unspoken words: *That's the guy who ruined the first dance.*

After-Action
Regret Meter: 10/10

Clean-up Cost: One wedding memory permanently scarred, and one lifelong ban from creamy pasta.

What I learned: Weddings are sacred. Buffets are dangerous. Combine them at your own risk.

Alex's wedding reception shame didn't mark the end of the week. Nature had its own plans – and they were much louder

---

10

NATURE CALLS. LOUDLY.

Camping is supposed to be peaceful, with a crackling fire, clear night sky, and the inviting smell of toasted marshmallows.

But when nature calls, peace quickly packs up and leaves.

My friends had invited me on a weekend camping trip, insisting it would be "good for the soul."

Fresh air, no phones, and bonding around the fire. I agreed, thinking it sounded relaxing. I brought a tent, a sleeping bag, and a cooler of snacks that could survive nuclear winter.

The first night was perfect.

We cooked hot dogs, told stories, and laughed under the stars. I felt almost like a rugged outdoorsman – until 3 a.m., when my stomach began growling in ways that had nothing to do with wolves. The chips and jerky I'd inhaled were staging a rebellion.

I stumbled out of the tent with a flashlight, trying not to wake anyone. The forest was quiet, except for the occasional hoot of an owl. I searched for privacy, found a decent patch of bushes, and crouched down.

That's when it happened.

The noise – loud enough to echo. In the stillness of the forest, it sounded like a tuba solo announcing my shame to every living creature within a mile radius.

My friends stirred in their tents. "Alex? You okay?" one of them called groggily.

I froze, mortified. "Uh...yeah! Just...checking the stars!"

The lie didn't hold.

By the morning, the story had spread around the campfire. My private disaster had become public entertainment. They reenacted it, mimicked the sound, and gave it nicknames. For the rest of the trip, every time an owl hooted, someone smirked and said, "Sounds familiar."

By the time we packed up and left, my dignity was buried somewhere in that forest. I could only hope the trees kept my secret. They didn't. My friends still bring it up on camping trips.

After-Action
Regret Meter: 8/10

*Clean-up Cost: One flashlight, one bush,
and endless reminders every camping season.*

*What I learned: The woods have ears.
And terrible acoustics.*

After surviving the wilderness, Alex faces a new kind of terror in a much more sterile environment.

11

THE MEDICAL EXAMINATION
MALFUNCTION

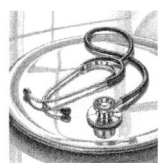

A nnual checkups are supposed to be routine. Quick in, quick out. A doctor pokes, prods, listens, nods, and you leave with a clean bill of health and maybe a reminder to eat more vegetables. That's how it was supposed to go.

For me, it turned into the kind of story my doctor will probably still be laughing about at retirement parties.

I'd prepared carefully. No coffee, no greasy breakfast, no mistakes that might throw off the bloodwork. Just a sensible snack a few hours before, so I wouldn't pass out. Thoughtful planning, right? Except that "sensible snack" was apparently plotting a medical coup. By the time I sat in Dr. Martinez's office, smiling and nodding politely while he reviewed my chart, my stomach was already negotiating its own treatment plan.

The first part went smoothly: Height, weight, blood pressure. A few questions about exercise and diet. I even bragged about how often I stretched, which was technically true if you counted reaching for the remote. Then we moved on to the physical exam.

"Hop up on the table," Dr. Martinez chirped.

And that's when my snack decided to make its presence known. Pressure built as he worked his way through the exam.

Reflexes? Fine. Breathing? Clear.

Everything seemed normal – except for the mounting storm in my gut.

Then came the abdominal exam. If you've never had one, here's how it goes: you lie flat, the doctor presses around your stomach, and you're supposed to stay relaxed while answering questions. That's it. Easy. Unless, of course, your digestive system is staging a full rebellion.

Dr. Martinez pressed gently. "Any tenderness here?"

I clenched, willed my body into silence, and managed a weak, "No."

He pressed again, lower this time. That was the trigger.

The sound that escaped was catastrophic. Not a polite squeak. Not a subtle whisper. It was a booming, unmistakable announcement that rattled the sterile room and left no doubt about what had just happened. And it wasn't just noise.

The smell hit instantly. Sterile medical air turned battlefield. I froze on the table, mortified. Dr. Martinez, a consummate professional, didn't flinch.

"These things happen more often than you might think," he said smoothly, like a man who had seen far worse and still had charts to finish. "Let's take a short break."

A short break. That meant paper towels, ventilation, and a quick change of underwear, courtesy of the emergency plastic bag the doctor discreetly handed me. I wanted to melt into the linoleum. Instead, I sat there, red-faced, while the doctor restored order to the exam room like nothing unusual had occurred.

We finished the checkup after the intermission, though neither of us mentioned what had happened. As I buttoned my shirt, Dr. Martinez handed me my paperwork and delivered his final advice with the calm authority of a man who had earned the right to speak truth.

"Alex," he said, "you're in good health overall. But my best advice today? Never trust a fart when someone is pressing on your abdomen."

I nodded, clutching the bag of ruined underwear like it was a scarlet letter.

Do not trust a fart, indeed.

After-Action Regret Meter: 10/10

Clean-up Cost: One ruined pair of underwear, one disinfected exam room, and one medical ego shattered.

What I learned: Doctors are trained for emergencies. That doesn't mean you should give them one.

Alex's medical disaster didn't end the week. At home, his smart devices were about to betray him – even worse.

12

THE SMART HOME BETRAYAL

S mart homes are supposed to make life easier. Voice-activated lights, automated reminders, and temperature just right. What they don't advertise is how quickly "convenience" can turn into "career sabotage."

I'd invested heavily – voice assistants, smart plugs, the works. My living room responded to me like I was Captain Kirk on the bridge of the Enterprise. Lights dimmed on command, music played instantly, and the thermostat listened better than most coworkers. It was futuristic. It was efficient. It was flawless.

Until the day of my big phone interview.

I'd applied for a dream job – better pay, more responsibility, actual benefits that didn't expire after three months. The interview was going well. I was nailing the answers, hitting the perfect balance of confidence and humility. For once, I felt like I belonged in the big leagues.

Then my smart assistant decided to chime in.

In the middle of my explaining how I'd successfully led a project rollout, a cheerful robotic voice cut through:

"Alex, you asked me to remind you about your regular appointment for STD screening at 3 p.m. today. Should I reschedule due to your current phone call?"

The silence that followed was deafening.

On the other end of the line, the hiring manager hesitated. I could practically hear him blinking. My career prospects now shared the stage with my very personal, very unnecessary medical reminders.

I scrambled. "Sorry – uh – my home assistant still doesn't understand privacy settings."

He chuckled politely, but we both knew what had just happened. We wrapped up with a hollow, "We'll be in touch soon," which sounded suspiciously like, "We will laugh about this at lunch and never call you again."

The rest of that day was spent angrily reprogramming the assistant's settings, muttering about betrayal, and wondering if I'd have to move to a cabin in the woods to escape technology.

The twist?

A week later, I received an email. I'd been shortlisted.

Apparently, the hiring manager appreciated my "commitment to responsible health practices" and "embrace of modern technology."

My humiliation had been recast as maturity. Who knew oversharing could pay off?

After-Action
Regret Meter: 9/10

Clean-up Cost: One job interview almost wrecked, and one "smart" home device deactivated.

What I learned: Technology listens. Sometimes, too well.

While technology nearly cost him a job, Alex's next blunder demonstrates that his own body could be just as traitorous as any smart home device.

13

WEDDING GUEST WIPEOUT

Weddings are supposed to be sacred. Holy vows, family tears, and carefully orchestrated beauty that people remember for years. They are not supposed to include me unleashing a brunch-fueled biological disaster during the most solemn moment of the ceremony.

Jane and David were college friends, and I was honored to be invited. The chapel was stunning: old stone arches, stained glass glowing in the afternoon sun, an organ playing softly as the bride walked down the aisle. Everyone leaned forward, smiling, tissues ready. It was the kind of ceremony that makes even cynics believe in romance.

The day had started with brunch. I should've known better. Champagne, omelets dripping with cheese, and an ill-advised second plate of sausages. It had seemed celebratory at the time. By the time Jane started her vows, it felt like all that food was staging its own wedding march through my digestive system.

I shifted in my pew, trying to stay composed. Deep breaths. Tiny adjustments. Maybe I could make it to the reception. Maybe I could hold on. But the chapel was silent, the acoustics flawless, and my body chose that exact moment to betray me.

The officiant had just said, "With this ring..." when it happened.

The sound bounced off the stone walls, echoing like someone had fired a starter pistol at the altar. Heads snapped around. Guests froze mid-breath. The bride faltered mid-sentence, eyes flicking toward the congregation with the kind of calm only politeness can provide.

And then the smell...

Sacred air transformed instantly. What had been a reverent silence was now one of shocked disbelief. A child giggled. An adult stifled a cough. My soul left my body, hovered near the stained-glass windows, and prayed for mercy.

The officiant, to his credit, didn't miss a beat. He plowed ahead, voice steady, as if nothing had happened. David focused fiercely on Jane, jaw tight, while Jane's eyes glimmered with the forced composure of a bride who would one day laugh about this – maybe.

I sat frozen, unable to move, certain everyone knew. The rest of the ceremony blurred. I couldn't clap, couldn't smile, couldn't look anyone in the eye.

When the final blessing ended, I bolted from the pew, skipped the receiving line, and drove home faster than you can say "uninvited."

I didn't go to the reception. I sent a gift by mail, a very generous one, hoping it might soften the memory of my "contribution" to their vows. Months later, Jane's thank-you card arrived.

It said: *"Unforgettable. Thank you for your memorable presence at our wedding."*

I wasn't sure if that was kindness. Or a warning.

After-Action
Regret Meter: 10/10

Clean-up Cost: One brunch, one friendship scarred, and one forever story in family folklore.

What I learned: Sacred silence and digestion don't mix. Skip the sausages.

Alex's chapel disaster wasn't the only humilia-

tion making headlines in his life. A train ride to work proved that technology can be just as cruel.

14

THE AUDIO APOCALYPSE

Morning trains are usually quiet places. People sip coffee, scroll news, or doze with their headphones on. It's a delicate peace held together by unspoken rules: no loud calls, no smelly food, no unsolicited noise. Which is why my mistake felt like dropping a grenade in a library.

My phone had been acting up for weeks – Bluetooth issues, random disconnects, the usual nonsense. I thought I had it under control. That morning, half-asleep, I opened a video message from my best friend Steve. He had a habit of sending ridiculous clips late at night, usually memes or fails; I figured it would give me a quick laugh before work.

I popped in my earbuds, confident they were paired. The train was silent. People read books, stared out windows, and nursed their lattes. Perfect time for a harmless chuckle.

Except my earbuds weren't connected.

The phone blasted the video through its external speakers at full volume. And not just any video. Steve, in his infinite wisdom, had sent me something... explicit. Very explicit.

The kind of sound that makes everyone in earshot instantly realize exactly what kind of video is playing, no matter how much you wish they didn't.

Moans. Gasps. Groans. Louder than the train itself.

Heads snapped up. Newspapers lowered. A woman clutched her child's shoulders and turned him away. My phone was announcing my shame to the entire car, and I fumbled like a man fighting off a live grenade.

It took ten eternal seconds to silence it. Ten. The longest ten seconds of my life.

When it finally stopped, the train was dead quiet again – except now everyone knew me as *that guy*. Some passengers stared at their shoes. Others smirked. No one said a word, but the silence screamed louder than the video had.

I stared at the floor until my stop, face on fire, praying I'd never see these commuters again. That afternoon, I bought wired headphones. Old-school. Reliable. Never betraying me in front of strangers.

Steve thought the whole thing was hilarious. Of course he did.

After-Action
Regret Meter: 9/10

Clean-up Cost: One commute destroyed, one phone nearly tossed onto the tracks, and one friendship under review.

What I learned: Never trust Bluetooth. And never trust Steve.

After disturbing the peace of a morning commute, Alex was about to prove that no location is safe from catastrophe.

15

CHURCH SERVICE CRISIS

C hurch is supposed to be peaceful. Reverent. The kind of place where you leave your distractions – and your digestive issues – at the door. For me – Alex – one Sunday morning proved that no amount of hymns or holy silence could drown out the betrayal of an ill-chosen breakfast.

I'd been going regularly for a couple of years. It was good for me: a little community, a little spiritual growth, a reminder not to be a terrible person during the week. That morning, I got dressed in my best church clothes, polished shoes, tucked-in shirt, and even a tie. I wanted to look the part. I wanted to belong.

The mistake? Brunch. Again. You'd think by now I'd have learned, but no; I showed up to service with champagne fizz still lingering in my gut, layers of sausage and eggs stacked like a Jenga tower, and a muffin that looked innocent but carried secret evil.

The service began beautifully. Opening hymns, a heartfelt prayer, and the warm hum of voices singing in unison. Pastor Williams set the tone with his steady presence, and the sanctuary filled with the kind of calm that makes you think, *Yes, this is what Sunday mornings are meant to be.*

Then came communion. The quietest, holiest part of the service. The music softened. The bread and wine passed carefully, row by row. People bowed their heads. The air itself felt sacred.

And that's when my stomach demanded to be heard.

I shifted in the pew, hoping to ease the pressure. Took a deep breath. Tried to convince my body to cooperate, just for five more minutes. Instead, it betrayed me spectacularly.

The sound wasn't small or polite; it was a booming announcement that ricocheted off the vaulted ceiling and stained-glass windows. If angels had been singing above, they stopped to listen. Heads lifted all across the congregation. Even the organist looked up, confused, hands frozen on the keys.

And you know what followed ...

Sacred air instantly corrupted. People coughed delicately into hymnals. A kid snorted out loud. I sat frozen, cheeks on fire, clutching the communion cup like it might grant instant forgiveness.

Pastor Williams didn't flinch. He looked out at the congregation, voice calm and steady: "Let us remember that we are all human beings, seeking grace together." His tone was gentle, inclusive, pastoral. But I knew. Everyone knew. His sermon had just acquired an unscheduled object lesson – and that object was me.

When communion ended, I slipped out quietly, avoiding the post-service handshakes and small talk. At home, I collapsed on the couch, certain that I had become permanent folklore in that sanctuary's history. And sure enough, weeks later, people were still referring to "the unforgettable Sunday."

Unforgettable, indeed.

After-Action

Regret Meter: 10/10

Clean-up Cost: One ruined suit, one brunch ban, and one spiritual reputation permanently scarred.

What I learned: Never test your faith and your colon at the same time.

Alex's holy humiliation wasn't the only betrayal that week. On a train ride, sleep – and drool – conspired to embarrass him again.

16

THE SLEEPING BEAUTY DISASTER

Trains are supposed to be relaxing. Scenic views, rhythmic clatter, maybe even a nap as you roll through the countryside. But when you share a car with strangers, relaxation can turn into regret in the time it takes for gravity to do its thing.

I was exhausted from a week of meetings and deadlines. The overnight train seemed like a blessing. I slid into my seat, nodded politely to the middle-aged businessman beside me, and settled in. He was quiet, courteous, and even respectful of the shared armrest. I thought: *Perfect. A considerate neighbor for the night.*

The train rocked gently. The lights dimmed. Sleep pulled me under fast.

When I woke, everything had changed.

My head was no longer upright. It was resting on my seatmate's shoulder. His very unwilling shoulder. And worse, my mouth had been open.

A wet patch gleamed on his sleeve. Large. Obvious. The unmistakable mark of drool.

I bolted upright, horrified. "Oh my God, I'm so sorry," I whispered, fumbling for tissues, wishing the train would derail just so I could escape.

The man gave a tight smile, dabbing at his sleeve with the kind of calm usually reserved for hostage negotiations. "No problem at all," he said.

Which translated roughly to: *I will absolutely tell everyone I know about this.*

The next three hours were torture. I sat rigid against the window, every muscle tense, determined not to move an inch. He slid his jacket between us as a barrier, subtle but unmistakable. I couldn't blame him.

By the time we pulled into the station, I had aged ten years.

He walked away quickly, probably eager to burn the shirt.

Me? I vowed never again to trust overnight trains – or at least to travel with someone who wouldn't mind being used as a human sponge.

After-Action
Regret Meter: 8/10

Clean-up Cost: One ruined shirt sleeve and three hours of silent shame.

What I learned: Sleep is bliss. Until it drools.

AFTERWORD

And there you have it: a collection of more than a dozen "please, God, let the ground swallow me whole" moments, lovingly documented so you can laugh without paying the price of living them yourself.

These are stories so spectacularly awful that you'll be retelling them at family dinners, office parties, and probably in a group chat before you've even finished the book.

If you laughed – chuckled, snorted, wheezed, or outright cried – then I've done my job. Life is heavy enough. Deadlines, bills, the news, all of it weighs on us.

Sometimes the only relief is humor – the kind that reminds us we're all ridiculous, fragile humans just trying to make it through the day without catastrophic digestive betrayal.

But it's not just laughter. These stories double as public service announcements. Let's be honest: if you were still naive enough to "let one slip" during a first date, a wedding ceremony, or an elevator ride, you've now been warned. Don't say I didn't prepare you.

And through it all, our hapless narrator, Alex, survives. Sure, he becomes folklore for all the wrong reasons. Sure, his reputation is in tatters across yoga studios, weddings, and workplaces.

But he still finds companionship, still gets work, still manages to wash his hands and keep moving.

That's the real takeaway: even when your body betrays you in the worst way imaginable, life goes on.

Sometimes smelly, sometimes mortifying, but always – *always* – worth laughing about later.

So let Alex be the stand-in for all of us – the unluckiest man in town, yes, but also a reminder that dignity can be rebuilt, and embarrassment fades faster than we think.

His disasters reassure us of one simple, universal truth: if he can survive all this, then there's hope for all of us.

Just remember the rule etched deep into this book, the one that might save you when the moment comes: **Don't. Trust. A. Fart.**

THANK YOU FOR READING THIS BOOK!

I would be incredibly grateful if you could take just 30 seconds to leave me a review!

Reviews are crucial for an author's livelihood, yet they can be surprisingly hard to get.

The more reviews my books receive, the more I can continue pursuing my love for creating books.

If you have any thoughts about this book, please leave a review and let me know.

- Sam

Printed in Dunstable, United Kingdom